SECOND THINGS

Also by Daniel Tobin

Poetry

Where the World Is Made
Double Life
The Narrows

Criticism

Passage to the Center: Imagination and the Sacred in the Poetry of Seamus Heaney

As Editor

The Book of Irish American Poetry from the Eighteenth Century to the Present
Light in Hand: Selected Early Poems of Lola Ridge
Poet's Work, Poet's Play: Essays on the Practice and the Art (with Pimone Triplett)

SECOND THINGS

DANIEL TOBIN

Four Way Books
Tribeca

Editorial Office
Four Way Books
POB 535, Village Station
New York, NY 10014
www.fourwaybooks.com

Library of Congress Cataloging-in-Publication Data

Tobin, Daniel.
Second things / Daniel Tobin.
    p. cm.
ISBN-13: 978-1-884800-88-7 (alk. paper)
ISBN-10: 1-884800-88-2 (alk. paper)
I. Title.
PS3570.O289S43 2008
811'.54--dc22

                                    2008017241

This book is manufactured in the United States of America
and printed on acid-free paper.

Four Way Books is a not-for-profit literary press. We are grateful for the
assistance we receive from individual donors, public arts agencies,
and private foundations.

This publication is made possible with public funds from
the National Endowment for the Arts and from the
New York State Council on the Arts, a state agency.

Distributed by University Press of New England
One Court Street, Lebanon, NH 03766

Contents

Fall   3

The Sea of Time and Space

The Tree   7
The Sea of Time and Space   8
Death and the Maiden   12
Vessels
    I.   *Mythos*   14
    II.   *Pleroma*   15
    III. *Logos*   16
    IV. *Kenosis*   17
Goat Song   18
Gilgamesh   19
Marduk   20
Lycanthropy   21
In the Bardo of Blue Light   23
Elegy for Smallpox   24
Disco Elegy   26
The Subway   27
Wherever You Happen to Be, There You Are
    I.   *Junior Moletch*   28
    II.   *The Local*   29
You Bet Your Life   30
Visitations
    I.   *Boy Waving from a Car, Kirkland St., 1983*   32
    II.   *Meteor Shower, Newton Drive-in, 1969*   34
    III. *Woman on a Train, Genoa to Paris, 1979*   36
    IV. *A Bee, Coney Island Nursing Home, 1963*   38
    V. *Wild Stallion, Point Reyes, 1977*   40

A Cone of the Eucalyptus

Crescendo		43
A Cone of the Eucalyptus		44
Yeats at Balscadden		45
And Singing Is All the Thought That Is in Them		
	I. *The Metra, The Muse*	46
	II. *For Christine at the Frost Farm*	47
Sketching the Galleries		
	I. *Floor Scrapers*	48
	II. *A Bather*	49
	III. *The Scream*	50
	IV. *Effigy Tumuli*	51
	V. *Piss Christ*	52
	VI. *The Holy Virgin Mary*	53
	VII. *Sun in an Empty Room*	54
Strategies for Turning Away		55
Transparencies		
	Body	58
	Soul	59
A Fable		60
In the Flesh		
	I. *Radial Keratonomy*	62
	II. *Wisdom Teeth*	63
	III. *Splinter*	64
	IV. *Mole*	66
	V. *Plantar Wart*	67
Senior Citizens' Polka		68
The Lay-Up		69
Say Grace		71
Weather Reports		
	A Red Leaf in Fall	73
	After	74

Garden Glosses
    I.   *Dead Nettle*   75
    II.   *Columbine*   76
    III.   *Delphinium*   77
    IV.   *Chives and Thistle*   78
    V.   *Stone Hare*   79
    VI.   *Forget-Me-Not*   80
    VII.   *Fiddlehead Fern*   81
Chin Music   82
Unchained Melody   86

OF THE HARMONY OF CELESTIAL REVELATIONS

Of the Harmony of Celestial Revelations
    I.   *The Reliquary*   91
    II.   *The Cell*   92
    III.   *The Sickness*   93
    IV.   *The Visions*   94
    V.   *The Language*   95
    VI.   *The World*   96
    VII.   *The Glass*   97
    VIII.   *The Healing*   98
    IX.   *The Greenness*   99
    X.   *The Music*   100
    Coda: The Garden   101
Fall Day   102

Notes   105

Our mind is disturbed when we try to plumb the depth of the world beneath us. But it reels still more when we try to number the favorable chances that must coincide at every moment if the least of living things is to survive and to succeed in its enterprises. After the consciousness of being something other and something greater than myself—a second thing made me dizzy: namely, the supreme improbability, the tremendous unlikelihood of finding myself existing in the heart of a world that has survived and succeeded at being a world.

—Teilhard de Chardin

FALL

The leaves are falling, falling
as from a great distance,
as though they had withered
in the sky's far gardens—

they fall with the look of someone
turning away.

And each night the earth
in its heaviness
falls alone
from the plenitude of stars.

All of us
are falling. This hand
falls. And these others,
it is in them all.

And, yet, there is One who holds
all this falling
forever, carefully, in his hands.

THE SEA OF TIME AND SPACE

THE TREE

Where it flung itself into the sky, its canopy
of leaves darkened three lawns, branches
flaring along the power lines, out and up
to fill the block's patch of heaven,
the trunk too thick to reach arms around,
which is why it's a legend to the neighbors
who like to tell how they cut it down
before we came, after the roots grew so big
they buckled their driveway's concrete slabs,
the ground that held its wide circumference
a wispy square of grass, the great bulk vanished
like my wife's father, once tall as a film star
in her salvaged photos, or myself
a child lifting my mother, wasted drunk,
off the floor to help her into bed.
It could be anything that has a hope
of giving life, though even the stump is gone,
ground to dust by deliberate hands. Below,
the thinnest hairs still widen, mesh
together, fanning out in blind passageways
to a source: some broken seal or outflow pipe
they quietly fill and fill to convey desire
toward nothing, an absence vast as their need.
And, suddenly, you're in the basement, grabbling
through the muck and wreckage of what you thought
swept effortlessly away. You are down on your knees.

THE SEA OF TIME AND SPACE

But we see only as it were the hem of their garments
When with our vegetable eyes we view these wondrous visions.
                                                    —Blake, "Milton"

I.

Midsummer, and a lone bee murmurs among the lavender
along the path we've laid into our garden,
round aggregate slabs that darken in rain
under the feathery leaves of the honey locust
whose lowest branches make us bow.
We have given the body the ritual of its need,
cooked *al dente, putanesca*, in the savory kitchen,
the tulip bowls of our glasses splashed with wine.
In after-dinner twilight still bright above the fence-line,
the compass angle of the house glows against the sky.
In such light, on Peckham Rye, Blake saw his first vision,
the tree above him filled with angels, their wings bespangled
with stars. Thereafter, prophets appeared in the fields
beyond Dulwich and Camberwell, Lambeth Vale;
Gabriel walked with him among the shambles at Carnaby,
his spirit guide through infinite London. And, one day,
God himself gazed from the casement window on Broad Street,
plain as a mother seeking her children in the crowd....
Our ancient days before this earth appeared to my mortal eyes:
inside each particle of dust the elemental strings,
behind the vegetable world the bleak Satanic mills—
gods of his own making, embodied states,
the titan walking behind the carapace of a flea.

II.

Single vision. The earth perceived merely as earth,
devoid of spirit's translucency, its light
dispersed in waves through the sea of time and space,
deranged by the gin of the unaltering eye....
One March morning, after making love, we saw
from our upstairs window a hint of green
among the brown scatter of leaves and wasted fronds
of fiddleheads, the first frail strips of crocuses,
like decorative ribbons, unblooming still,
until earth's economy compounded the scales
in hyacinth and candy-tuft, in phlox overbrimming
the steps, starbursts in the slow motion of its falls.
For weeks we found sprigging among the beds
pliant trunks of infant maples, their outsized
leaves spreading like river deltas, gathering light.
And we'd go uprooting, feeling in our hands the tug
of generation, its mechanism and miracle,
incessant fall of the eternal driven from sweet delight,
unless the mind revive and the body wash itself
of experience. All spring we listened to squirrels
in heat along the power lines, to the sparrows'
untraceable clamor through the trees.
You soaped aphids from the flutes of honeysuckle,
scattered shards of eggshells under the hostas
to guard them from the slugs you swore you heard
chewing each night through the darkened canopy,
their soft bellies bleeding on quicksilver trails of slime.

III.

In the suburbs of Ulro the mills whirr into motion—
Case, Modine, Twin Disc, plush furnaces of Metal World.
Invisible occupants swag in the burdened clouds.
Their poisons silver the leafage after rain,
sift into soil and skin, ineradicable, resurrect
in the brute lump seething in the mother's breast.

Strange smells along the lakeshore, North Beach closed
again beyond the Treatment Plant. Under dead stacks
at Cliffside the church league softballers shout
for their buddy rounding third and heading home.
He has become the idea he longed himself to be
before the grind, and slides safely into reclaimed dirt.

Now, along Franklin Street—call it New Poverty Lane—
under the shadow of the genius's office tower
(his leaking monument to Nature and to Work),
the settled migrant walks beside his ramshackle home,
labors to fulfill the alderman's injunction
to beautify the town or face a fine.

This evening, in the garden, we released the last
of the ladybugs, our small effort at harmony,
their killing a necessary hunger in the balance.
And now, at the feeder, a congregation of birds
pecks at the seed. They bolt, and a jackdaw assumes
the roof, fixed eye unblinking. He caws and caws.

IV.

Today, as though all life existed to amaze us,
a dragonfly alighted on the bench where you were sitting,
gold as though daubed in golden ink, and stayed
a full five minutes, motionless as a brooch.
When Blake descended to his garden, *A Human Wonder of God,*
he'd sit naked with his wife in full view of the street,
as though their bodies had passed into translucency,
light shining through the portal of every pore.
Upstairs, the graver's tools, copper plate and burin,
took ease of their labors in the mind's illuminations:
as though, as though, until what the soul longs for
scores itself within the body's finite bounds—
creation hieratic in its web of incarnation.
Playing on their trampoline, the neighbor children shout.
Another neighbor's falcon squawks inside its cage.
Blue globes of thistle shake mildly in a breeze.
The roses, past their bloom, bleed like wax into their stems.
On his deathbed, Blake sang a favorite childhood hymn,
then disappeared, as he said he would, into "The Next Room."
Just now, as if in unison, the fireflies ascended,
emanations of the Mundane Shell, or drifting stars?
No, they are our small lanterns waking with the night.
Just now, just now, and now it is just then.
We might be under water with the bergamot and hyssop.
And the bee remains a pilgrim, aloof and prodigal,
still humming to the engines of his own bright world.

DEATH AND THE MAIDEN

The spastic woman in her wheelchair tries
not to flail her arms as if she were falling,
as Nietzsche said, in all directions at once,
or so the professor in the balcony considers
while his wife leans over to him to remark
how the second violinist looks kind of cute—
something about his eyes—before the bow
strikes its note and she hands him the glasses.
But now already the strings are unfurling
their fury, *allegro, andante con molto,* as Death,
his jet hair moussed to a widow's peak,
designer Ray-Bans doubling the maiden's face,
his face caught with hers in her eyes' wide stare
moves in to seduce her. Already the boy in back
has stopped fumbling his bag of smuggled chips.
Already his too-patient father has forgotten
the tenor of his warnings. Death has a sleek car,
and a yacht in the harbor. Death has a mansion
in the Italian Alps, a summer house in Provence,
a private island that the woman down front,
drifting off in her fur, glimpses through a mist
she mistakes for sleep. By now the violist
has forgotten his clash with the first violin
over what to play that evening. By now the cellist
has suppressed his reverie of the compost pile
on the farm he plans for his retirement upstate.
The *scherzo, allegro molto,* whirls among the audience
like so many bright leaves, and they see,
in the moment, that Death has lit her cigarette,
that Death is running his fingers through her hair
while the professor and his wife sit with their coats

between them, and the woman in her wheelchair
waves her arms like a conductor and *presto,*
the maiden's lips part, and the musician's hands,
so precise and turbulent, go still.

VESSELS

I. *Mythos*

In the beginning was the hand, opposable,
little god's head of a fist,

the star-shape of its mouth—toothless,
sidereal—hurling its curses

into the void. The hand wants to be
an oracle, to bestow

on the world its five-fold wisdom,
glossolalia of wants,

always the eyeless face looking
to strike. *Open, open,*

the prayer goes up. And the god
lies down in its emptiness.

II. *Pleroma*

To go beyond the human
cannot be signified....

But then what good
is it for us who have
no such significance
and too much?—language:

      its torn effulgence.

On this side the soul
flung free of the burning;
on that side the scintilla
at the atom's center:

      zero without bounds.

On that side a light
that is its own prism;
on this side the body
like a fish in neon:

      aswim in its wants.

And in between: *pleroma*,
word dropped, plumb-line,
into the emptiness
stretched world to world.

III. *Logos*

Here is language,
a valise we carry
in our mouths.

It is traveling
with us—do you see?—
not like a pet
in its plastic cage,
moaning in stowage
begging to be

set free. It *is*
us, errant
in the circuitry.

What shall we say
to it, fellow traveler
in the bones,
is there anything
it doesn't know?

Off the tongue
words roll
like baubles:

mountain, snowdrift.

And in the throat
the breath
shuts tight.

IV. *Kenosis*

Snake that sheds
its skin until
there is only skin
and no snake,
and the skin is this
living world.

Holy, Holy, Holy
God without
power or might.
Out of you all
things pour until
you are nothing—

a desire bedded
into the body's
lush ciphers,
sweet absence
where you touch us
now and now and now.

GOAT SONG

It's as though the soul
were ghost writer
composing scenes
for the play of your life.

And you're the star,
stunned in the last act
by the blind fact
that you are who you are:

someone who's witnessed
his world renounced,
the sham announced
by roving chorus.

Oh let Oedipus
wear the sackcloth
and gouged eyes for truth's
apotheosis—

tragedies are soaps.
Gaze clear-eyed at what
the fates serve up,
confident knowing

that even if you've
married your mother
and murdered your father
you did it for love.

GILGAMESH

When I was king of kings and knew
every virgin I thought my due—
a city-full—and nobles' wives,
no one I fought came back alive.
I'd lord it inside those walls
whose every brick bore my name.
Even the gods obeyed my call
when I'd pray for—what else?—more fame
and they sent me my twin.
Nothing would be the same again

when Enkidu and I roved out
to prove ourselves. The sun's clout
affirmed us. We snuffed like bulls
in battles till the destined one fell
and I was left to know how gods
hated themselves in us, hated
our arrogance, the fire in our blood
like theirs—hated what they made.
Was my fate fated or chosen?
And how could I go back again

to what I was? Wearing his clothes
I became my brother, a hero
bent on the last plunge of my quest:
to pluck a rose from the sea of death.
What could the plant have been but life,
the losing of it, history?
Home, I preached it's also life
to be satisfied with a story
that renews itself like snakeskin:
in your life my death is born again.

19

MARDUK

Here is the true adamant and will of the world:
out of my mother's body I made the world.

To cut her in two as though gutting a fish,
that is one recipe for making a world.

From her eyes empty rivers, from her breasts mountains,
from the wound of my birth, the release of the world.

The snows are her siftings, each breeze her last breath
that wanders the roads like the lost of the world.

To save them from loss I raise up my cities,
each one a beacon, a map of the world.

On streets I have left no place for the errant
for in every home I alone light the world.

If the gods want to sleep, I will let them sleep
and make myself god, the lord of this world.

I am the grain, the plough cleaving its furrow.
I am the storm that floods the whole world.

I am the singular, and the dispersal.
I judge all the living and dead of the world.

These words were judged by god's judge and given:
whispers through walls, wind, another world.

LYCANTHROPY

For his life he can't remember when it happened:
on that dank Transylvanian heath,
fog machines cranking full-blast;
or behind the hermaphrodite's tent at Carnival,
his girl drifted into the crowd,
Teutonic peasants in folk costumes
prancing through the eerie streets;
or was it in his sleep, that recurrent dream
no longer dreamt because lived?
Anyhow, one morning he found the scar
beneath his left nipple, over his heart,
though at the time it seemed more birthmark than bite.
Before long he's rooting through woods with gypsies
who recite bad poems in backs of wagons:
Even a man who is pure in heart
and says his prayers by night,
may become a wolf when the wolfbane blooms
and the moon is full and bright.
More moon-obsessed than Keats,
he notes the orb's every nuance, knowing
somehow his fate waxes with its glow;
sees archetypes everywhere, pentagrams
in the palms of his friends' hands: a wolf,
teeth bared, leaping through a star of David.
His girl leaves him for a handsome bürgermeister,
athletic except for his missing left arm,
lost in the Battle of the Balkans.
This, and the full moon, pull him over the edge:
he grows suddenly hairier, makes trouble
by tearing several of the townsfolk to pieces.
They hunt him in packs—clubs, pickaxes

waving in air, until the bürgermeister,
afraid he might want his girl back,
shoots him with a silver bullet. It's dark.
Only he sees the man's transformation
back to his old self in death. A mistake,
the townsfolk agree. Besides, who would believe
the beast was a favorite son? They carry him
to his father, the baron, who blames it all
on himself. Why had he not married again
after the boy's mother ran off with a vampire?
He calls an analyst, has his fears confirmed.
Still no one can fire into his own heart the bullet
of illumination. Exeunt all, except the old gypsy
who lags behind, keening in fogged moonlight.
In the tragic world there are no sequels,
only the same events repeated *ad infinitum*
in other lives with additional assorted monsters,
and no mad doctor to alter the structure
of the infected brain, and hence the story,
so the moon again is looked upon in innocence.

IN THE BARDO OF BLUE LIGHT

That man rooting through graveyards, sewing
the parts of dead men together till his creature
wails menacingly above him, the man dragging
proudly on his cigarette in the afterglow
of the bomb sight, do they bring good things
to light? It's the heartbeat of America
that calls to you rush hours on the car phone,
heat waves billowing above the pavement—
Marilyn's dress in *The Seven Year Itch*.
Or, alternatively, it's the real thing
reflected in the eyes of a homeless man
begging dollars on Broadway, blaming inflation
for the increase, his dream like yours
everywhere you want to be. Have it your way,
he says, gnashing his teeth while you
walk blankly past, his fists two stones
unable to fling themselves at the sky.
You, too, would rather discover yourself
here than run for the border, your true voice
like a pear tree new each morning,
all the sweet fruit waiting to be picked.
Fresh is the taste, but not after Eden—
that bedroom where nightly you cup your hands
to your face to drink your own tears,
baleful, bitter, and good to the last drop.

ELEGY FOR SMALLPOX

This is how Pandora would have done it
had gods given her a rubber suit
protective as their own accustomed wont
of changing into what they would repute,
the rattle-box clicked shut without remorse
for we would have history otherwise.

So it's no surprise to see this doctor
decked out to moonwalk, devout as a priest,
the petri dish a ritual offered
at the shrine of the holy of holies;
though really, he's the executioner
who would flick the switch on the bland killer

while outside cheer millions of blistered ghosts.
Surely among them some unknown girl
fights back memories, those days host
to compresses, bloodlettings, her skin a hail
of sores wrapped tight in scarlet blankets,
the light itself scarlet—what's left of it—

glimpsed in a delirium of drapery,
the color itself become a salve.
Mummified Ramses, fevered in Egypt,
died. No prayers, litanies of *Aves*,
could have spared him, or the virtuous emperor
at whose death chaos spread like plague through Rome.

Invisible on air, the blind angel
takes wing, ignoring the signs, the deeds
fostered in fear civilizations ago,
until it's leashed miraculously
here, *an entity on the borderline*
between the living and non-living,

to remind us of our own depths
of possibility, of what still could be
though we press the button on our worst
incarnation, and a thousand centuries
evaporate—ash: Tear down the red curtains,
the god is dead. Tear those curtains down.

DISCO ELEGY

You were barely old enough to drive
And gave your pulsing body to the beat.
All you wanted was to stay alive,

To let the primal rhythm's pounding tide
Wash over you and guide your flagrant feet.
You were barely old enough to drive

To "Fifty-Four," "2001"—sexual hives
Throbbing through the night, those bodies
Sweating, passionate to stay alive.

A stud in heels and chains, hair blow-dried,
You strutted like Travolta down the street,
A cock of the walk on overdrive,

And did The Hustle, The Bump and Grind,
The dance floor pumping its collective heat
Under a flashing ball—*Stayin' Alive!*

Oh it was kitsch, but who wouldn't reprise
Innocence awash in its churning sea,
Those first days of being old enough to drive.
All you wanted was to stay alive.

THE SUBWAY

We made a ring around him, Buddha in a polo shirt
at the platform's center reading someone's palm:
"You will live to a hundred and gain great wealth,"
he spoke to a smirking teen who, with the rest of us,

descended to this realm of caged bulbs, shuttered
news stands. Despite our shrugs he remained serene,
mirrored our laughter back; though when he turned
to me, and took my hand to scrutinize the lines

I felt a charge along my arm, then heard his judgment:
"You won't live so long, but you'll gain enlightenment."
My friend twirled his finger, mouthed a theremin,
while our homebound train ramrodded into the station—

leaving me to ask what to make of it all: my life
something less than light along a rail, a bright
gliding of wheels, only a rumble below a grate—
the sudden, freshening wind of something passing.

WHEREVER YOU HAPPEN TO BE, THERE YOU ARE

I. *Junior Moletch*

Whoever he was he key-scratched his name
into the building's third floor landing sign
beside our apartment door, though no one
of all that lost world's swirling whispers
ever heard of him, or paid any mind
to his bland remembrance, more defacement,
except me, who had no reason to care
but that the name sounded pure cartoon
to a ten year old who'd assumed his turn
before the schoolyard's squad of taunting faces
only to seize the gauntlet himself, feeling
the pleasure of another's brokenness,
hurt shining in the eyes, polished steel—
all of it almost forgotten in the gloss
of survival. And Junior, proud Junior,
whoever he was, still nowhere to be found.

II. *The Local*

"Get off here and you're in Jewville," the boy
says to his companions, all of them decked
out in elephant-wide pants and jock shoes.
They blustered on at the last stop—*cronies*
my father would have called them in his time,
loudmouths, wiseguys, though they're not *toughs*
or *gangbangers,* not one more than fourteen,
and bound, maybe, for someone else's bad news
should their track roll on from slur to switchblade,
their school packs inked with *gangsta* rap logos.
At their age I'd have leather patches stitched
to my Levis, so cool I could have quick-drawn
my fuck-you finger at anyone not my kind,
preening in the role my birthright afforded me:
no *homeboy* but a boy too charged by home,
like anybody with baggage better left behind,
another someone from somewhere with nowhere,
only his own world in his head. Through this train's
sealed windows key-scratched with names
station after station lurches into place.

YOU BET YOUR LIFE

The meek man wearing horn-rimmed glasses,
could have been my first nightmare teacher
from high school, or that sad-sack contestant
I saw on reruns of *You Bet Your Life*.
Instead, he's the subject of that film
in Psych 101, an experiment
in which the hidden camera lingers
on his face as he presses the button
that fires the needle, mock electric shocks
jolting the actor in the booth next door
whose feigned screams grow savage
as the meter jumps higher, the man
unmoved in his resolve. My friends and I
tried that experiment, our first subject
a girl I'd broken up with. She sat
in the jerry-rigged room pressing the button,
watching a video of me twitching at each shock,
then rocking as the mock charge grew more intense
until, sobbing, shaking, she bolted from the room.
Who knows what she was thinking—something
about loss, how I pressured her for sex,
then left her? Or was it pain rising
like magma in the throat, a brute cry
that's swallowed or lashes out?
It's nothing I tell myself, that stab
she must have felt when her worst
impulses found their brief fulfillment.
That's when I see her hugging her husband
as she leaves for work—shy Terry, undamaged,
who maybe heard three bodies fall to the floor
one bad day in her freshman year when cruelty

was easy as a game show: my friends and I
blind and stammering in the hall, barely breathing,
slapping our sides as if stifling flames, laughing like hell.

VISITATIONS

I. *Boy Waving From a Car, Kirkland St., 1983*

Distraught by the weather
of who he is, he moves
among the fraying crowd,

heedful only of their part
in his world's injustice.
Shadows start at his feet,

ghost each fraught step.
Nothing can assuage
his *cri de coeur*

that ripens, a fruit,
to bursting. Dantesque,
he would devolve

from that pinnacle,
heaven's kaleidoscope
whirling him back

to the wood in which
he wanders now, clichéd.
And the girl he misses

sends no angel in answer,
having divined all this
from his eagerness to be

wherever she would be;
whatever, perversely, she
would have him be.

His gut clenches
as he turns up the street,
the small hand reaching

to pluck what grows
inside, the car speeding
faster, speeding away.

II. *Meteor Shower, Newton Drive-In, 1969*

Memory has them
teeming down from on high,
sudden above the bright horizon
of the screen whose images
  float, pixel-titans

  blind to their fate,
  which is, like everything,
to go blank. No wonder, seeing them—
  bottle rockets streaking
    soundless in descent—

  the father's moved
  to tell his son, and motions
with his hand that for a moment
  darkens the patina of light
    that paints his face,

    hypnotic-blue sheen.
  Such might have been the gaze
of the stunned soldiers at Sardis
  confronted by the miracle:
    a fixed star rocketing

  breakneck across
  the firmament, its trail
a fabulous blazonry of hair.
  And so the battle stops,
    and scribes recount

the god's decree.
Less once sparked a child's awe
beyond the sublunary's greater glow,
to count them in his own
book of wonders.

III. *Woman on a Train, Genoa to Paris, 1979*

An apple in the palm, the gift
offered, arm bent like a branch
below the woman's breast, no,
it's a tendril, for the fruit's
the center, and the man's hand
blossoms also from its flesh
forming, as in Cranach, her perfect
complement, their sexes hidden
behind bunches of grape leaves,
the beasts consumed in postures

of thought. So they both hold
the apple in his mind that moment
before the paring knife starts
its work, and the landscape—
Loire, Auxere—bereft of allegory,
blurs, brushstrokes of blue,
green, and gold in the spotted
window. She moves nearer him
on the seat while the others
in the compartment fade to gray

as in some cloying film that ends
with the chance rendezvous come
to enduring love. But he's too shy,
too taken with his own teasing fear
to seize the day, though he's far
from home, far from anyone
who would have a say. So she fades

into the panoply, her face smooth
as the fruit on Cranach's Tree,
its web of roots spreading underground.

IV. *A Bee, Coney Island Nursing Home, 1963*

Bulk a striped hairshirt of chitin and fuzz,
the flimsy see-through wings barely bear him up
while he cruises the chain-link, tubby angel
whose charges are these weeds flowering
from concrete. Though really, it's fancy
to see it so, for it's hungry, hungry
with its own charge from the hive.
And if by happenstance of grace these buds
come to claim this meager strip of grass,
it's only from surfeit of instinct, chance
profit of a lottery turned by no hand.
Maybe that's why—though as yet he knows
mostly kinder tales grown-ups tell to quiet thought—
the small boy races breakneck from the fence
as if to flee some terror in a labyrinth,
fearing the creature's legendary bite;
and falls as he flees, knees scraped on the lot
he wished was midway at Steeplechase,
its raucous rides, cacophony of calls,
faces vivid in the spotlight of event,
soon fading in the flicker-trail
of memory: anything but this weekly trip
he's only coming to comprehend—
the Sunday drive down ritual streets,
hallways cured with bleach, a bone-white room,
the clammy strangeness of his grandfather's hand
barely raised from bed. And this bee,
the boy's stunned, humiliating screech
that thins to nothing in the room above

where nurses turn the old man for his shot
under the ceiling light's fluorescent buzz.

V. *Wild Stallion, Point Reyes, 1977*

Sky and sky. And after sky, a space flight's integers
   of wonder. And after: visionless distance
more penetrating than this headland, its sea-cliffs
   rampant with the wind's scrawls, the ocean
foaming ashore, awash in its slow eternity; distance
   that is itself impenetrable, that is,
useless, except as furthest backdrop for this wood
   where he walks beneath stanchioned redwoods—
wispy beard, backpack snug to his shoulders, the path
   opening on more path, on the promise
of expanse, his dream of the west a dream of revelation.

Behind him: the Greyhound's hum, hitchhiked rides
   from Famine's End to Tamalpais,
those cult recruiters who approached him on the Wharf,
   their lies nearly alluring; further north,
a Renaissance Fair where he picked from motley crowd
   that friend who took him further back—
concrete yards of apartments, row houses, malice
   of voices through a bedroom wall,
haunts that flowed with smuggled beer, boy-talk.

Here is hunger of vision, livid under the trees'
   spidered canopy, as now, from somewhere
up the path he hears the rhythm of hoof beats growing
   louder, dithyrambic. And it flashes
past, ashen, its mane driven behind as it gallops
   toward granite boundaries, scrub-pine,
windscape, crashing sea. There, too, he'll stand
   dumbstruck, wanting to carry it
with him, wanting to leave it behind—his life.

A CONE OF THE EUCALYPTUS

CRESCENDO

It starts with a screech, a howl,
the brute's pure note
guarding its kill, sweet wail
as loins lock to further the line,
a fossil's plaint diminished in stone.

Only slowly, painstaking, tenacious,
are words shaped around the sounds,
the true range to be staked out
in arias, each mastered stage,
until, in achieved splendor,

a man stands dazzlingly alone
amidst the spectacle, the music
an horizon arranged about him,
his mouth holding eternally the O
in which silence empties itself into song.

A CONE OF THE EUCALYPTUS

So many piled beneath the peeling tree
it seems a late polluted hail had come,
some antediluvian, post-biblical plague
that fell and fell and blotted out the sun
and would not melt, but scattered like leaves

across the walk where you bend down, pick one,
then place it squarely in my palm. "Look, Dan,
at the star-shape on the crown, the hollow cone
a bloom of five born out of four." And soon
you're quoting sages—Plato and Thomas Browne—

"the quincunx blossoming from quaternity":
such mystical symmetries, to which you add
bodies in the Kaballah, the Tarot, the Torah,
Christ on the Cross, snowflakes, the human hand.
I run my thumb along the pith. Four scars

ascend to where something—call it nature—
fixed hull to crest, each rough plane perfected
like a fossil browned by centuries in earth,
and five carved points that open into black,
and look like a seal, and are deeply cured.

Mark, my *reb*, whose name doubles wisdom,
you could convince me to believe in Blake
and his eternity, a heaven encased in words;
this shell the image my own soul might make,
its wounds at seed under bone-white boughs.

YEATS AT BALSCADDEN

He labored above the impassable coast
where gulls hovered to their nests on rock,
shy youth worrying his dream-drenched songs.
He wandered below the Ben of Howth,
his self-conscious cloak flapping in a wind
that lifted the bracken's leathery fronds
in twilight descending on Ireland's Eye
and the gas-lit city he would come to hate

near sixty years on, its "*paudeen*" streets
a pastiche of his filthy modern tide,
hum of streetlamps' pale, redundant moons
drowning the ghost-lit music of the spheres
where he stood alone on O'Connell Bridge.
Months from his own new moon, all masks
dropped, he confessed his rage at what he saw
and prayed for a third war to wipe the slate.

Forgiving himself the lot, he may be back,
a strange tourist of the new millennium
milling among the *nouveau riche*, a chorus
of cell phones perched in their hands singing
of what is to come, while the new estates
spread inexorably toward the summit.
He sees the fierce rocky faces of these cliffs
still plummeting into the stone-revising sea.

AND SINGING IS ALL THE THOUGHT THAT IS IN THEM

I. *The Metra, The Muse*

I hardly recognized her—the pants suit,
the prim hair, the London Fog raincoat
draped across her lap, and nearly missed
the voice for all the shunting of the car:

This train is Zeno's arrow that never
meets its mark, Einstein's elevator
rocketing through space, its trace
your furtive eyes. So take quick note
of the Golden Nugget off Ravenswood,
its stack of neon pancakes on the roof;
remember the Goodbye Wall outside
Clybourn Public Storage, its portraits
of lost species fading under fumes.
Keep everything you've caught these mornings
in their attitudes of departure....
Let the conductor nick your ticket.
Believe the sun prints its watermark through clouds.

II. *For Christine at the Frost Farm*

(Ripton, Vermont)

The master's cabin's overrun by mice
or something bigger that's dragged your store
of fresh-ground coffee across the floor
    as though it were the poet's teasing trace

of something dark and deep that had gotten in
from the woods outside, leaving its small scats
on the linen. You say you'll make the best
    of it, long-distance, on the phone.

Hearing you, I find myself fending away
my own slinking pest inside, the creature
cringing in solitude's bleak nest; or worse,
    that shadow transfigured by the urge to save,

and purge all impediment to your hunger—
words laid down, a bright trail from your life.
Follow it farther than you can see now, love,
    awake all night, spying the miles to go.

SKETCHING THE GALLERIES

I. *Floor Scrapers*

What do you make of that odd one by the door,
his silk top hat and greatcoat folded
neatly beside his chair, a sketchbook flapped
over his knees, and his eyes: flint-gray, steady—
someone staring down his own death?

To him we are the shapes our bodies make
around themselves, the *scratch, scratch* of charcoal
ferreting its trail across the blank page.
When he is finished, will he have captured
the glisten of sweat down our shirtless backs,

the taut press of our arms at the work?
I think we will be like these ringlets, stripped
layers of pigment curling into themselves,
the window behind a frame of absence,
the floor, the whole room, awash in light.

But to be as stubbornly here as this stain!
Do you see? It's not him anymore but others
crowded there, and you and I before them
whispering together, confidantes:
Soon, soon this canvas will be white again.

II. *A Bather*

She could be doubled
over in pain, bending low
to scrub some spot from the wash-
tub that, oddly, could be a
frying pan the way the perspec-
tive tilts everything towards the
viewer and away from those
tousled bed sheets, the blurred
hieroglyphs on the rug. Her own
face has disappeared into
the anonymity of light
gracing her skin, her pinned-
up hair, the soft rise
of her hips that hides
her sex. The faintest touch
of wind could disturb
these blue curtains, the wet
residue in this great round basin
she cannot get clean enough.

III. *The Scream*

The man's head is a light bulb
from which the landscape rises like heat,
his nose a skull's halved ellipsis,
the eyes a pair of melting stones.

His mouth is the "o" in the word *alone*,
his hands barring the sound from his ears.
If he could he would rewind the whole
frantic dash across this bridge

that never ends—the two girls ambling
indifferently behind, and, far off,
those boats in the bright lap of the bay
that have set sail to the vanishing point.

IV. *Effigy Tumuli*

Wasted mesa. Earth stripped to bleeding mounds
where miners' claws gouged the venerable clay.
Here, among shucked barrens of pyrite and shale
the river wearies, slowing to shallows.

Along earth-moved hummocks the eye charts
an exploded view—a pad's vague carapace,
a rift's jagged writhe—aching to make whole
the shattered forms. I stand back, effaced,

waiting to be lifted, the way Black Elk
in a vision quest climbed over cities,
for a moment loss shading into wonder:
Water-strider. Frog. Catfish. Turtle. Snake.

V. *Piss Christ*

Between urine and feces,
so even strict Augustine
believed the savior entered
the body of the world.

Likewise this artist,
his God risen again
in the golden shower
of our waste ascending.

Let the politicians
and philistines
lick their chops,
another crucifixion.

They have no place
in so replete a rapture.

VI. *The Holy Virgin Mary*

Outside the crowd wants beauty,
an icon daubed in gold, the pure
mother they've grown accustomed to,
all whiteness and descending doves.
Inside what they cannot fathom,
this effigy composed of earth,
glides across her canvas, face
a goddess's tutelary mask,
one breast a sacred mound of dung—
the demon they fashion out of night.
A host of labial butterflies
pursue their circuit where she floats,
though cries and prayers rise up against
this holiness envisioned here.

VII. *Sun in an Empty Room*

Light that makes walls these various shades of milk
pours through this open window,
and what might be outside—you can't see it—
could be all you'd ever care to know of beauty.

If you lived here, you'd do your best
to furnish their emptiness with precious things—
luminists in which the spacious scene
appears poised to ascend, or a portrait of yourself

sketched to nervous laughter on the boardwalk.
Though why not a Fra Angelico, that courtyard
where the Virgin, a lady in waiting,
receives the angel with his brightly-colored wings?

Or maybe it's a summer cottage where you wait
for family, friends, for everyone to arrive.
It might be any variety of heaven,
though it seems everything's been taken away—

these bare white walls, a floor so spare
it could be in pain. This is the house the sun lives in
like an old man who has nothing left, or a mind
brushed to transparency, the only place you wish to be.

STRATEGIES FOR TURNING AWAY

Morning. He nuzzles more deeply
into the pillow. White. White.
This is the first strategy,
to make of his face a stone,
worm's shelter, shelter of earth.
Already its heaviness prints the ground.

*

As he drives to work he envies
the pavement's infinite patience,
how it accepts anything—
traffic's incessant swish and moan,
blown tires, oil slicks, skid tracks,
a dead dog's mash of blood
and fur, earth's indifference
working up through the cracks,
the steamroller's slow, suffocating press.

*

Outside his office window
the lake churns like new cement,
each swift upsurge over the berm
a fanfare of spray slapping rock.

Like a writ that surfaces
years after it's composed,
he remembers how, in Eckhart,
the heart devises

out of its own earthly needs
strategies for turning away
from what it most desires—
the divine names inscribed,

a code through all things:
light, and *good* and *beautiful*.
And, welling at the bottom
of the self's dull pool, *ecstasy*.

*

Once in a museum he saw a mask,
fierce visage of a god the man
who wore it would become amidst
dances, chants—an alchemy of words.
Though it's wrong to say the man
became the god and ceased
to be himself: who danced
in that distant village was a God-Man.

*

As in Goya where the colossus,
all gaping mouth and eyes,
tears through its own son's flesh
as through a smaller version of itself,

so he pictures himself holding
the child he was in his hands,
its scream disappeared in echoes of ink,
the ripped-open body gnawed like a sleeve.

*

The evening news with its rattle-bag
of horrors, litanies of pain—
he always turns away,
flicks to another station
where a stunned man shambles
between mirrors, his likeness
a paper cut-out unfolded to infinity
so it's impossible to say
which is image, which is real.

He loves that film, how in the end
the camera pans over the warehouse,
vast jigsaw, until it lingers
on the beloved: discarded
childhood sleigh, the one piece
that would complete the puzzle.

That's when he realizes
the viewer is like the dead
who see everything whole,
his own life a whispered name
drifting in smoke above the furnace.

TRANSPARENCIES

*If the eye were a living creature
its soul would be its vision.*

—Aristotle

Body

To be precise it must be like the split-
second when a rose burgeons from its bud
or water boils, though without the requisite
rumbling inside the kettle's hollow dome
to signal the beholder; but being there,
wherever absence crackles into sight,
ought to fix us certainly as a star,
even if to say so is fancy, and flight
is more the way the world makes manifest
the many of what it is: a camera
flash, paparazzi swarmed into a host,
the scientist bent before the chimera
in the dish, all shudder as the flow
stands still, and the eye rounds itself to zero.

Soul

The proverbial eye, Aristotle's trope
for showing what we are, depends on form.
So each soul assumes its place, its proper
pinnacle. So worlds amass in vision's atoms.
And it's not just the human. Oak and ax
have their bourne too, the one to grow toward light,
the other with its dream of calloused hands
lifting it to the trunk as though for flight.
Which is why the warrior names his sword,
the child his imaginary friend.
We need a world intent and animate
to bring us otherwise back to ourselves,
lover and lover lying down, the spirit
awash and content in the body's knowledge.

A FABLE

It happens after a great feast, Body
collapses on a couch, limp as a pair of overalls.
Why should we take it anymore, Brain whispers,
just loud enough for others to hear,
that gas-bag getting fat on our hard work.

In no time Teeth, gnashing, break ranks.
In rebellion, Fingers flex into fists.
Even Toes are in conclave. Penis
rears his head and shouts *I can stand
on my own!* The Belly defends itself,
mustering only a few faint gurgles—
the sound of a man submerged.

You have to imagine what happens next,
Body in resentment withholding food,
Legs dancing jigs of liberation,
Mouth singing palinodes to freedom,
and Brain, who started it all,
mulling over big plans for everyone.

Pretty soon: gnawing. How quickly
the clamor dies down. Brain thinks,
Maybe this wasn't a good idea. So Body
begs forgiveness, though the Belly
will have none of it. Picture the voracity
of the Belly's wrath, Body tearing
hungrily at itself, Eyes bulging like onions,
Teeth—so many hard candies—
scattered across the floor, Genitals

a basket of rotten fruit. Brain,
that dried walnut, shrivels into itself.

But look at how big the Belly has grown,
raising its dome over the wasted limbs.
Look at all the buzzing angels descending.

IN THE FLESH

Five minor wounds

I. *Radial Keratonomy*

The metal clamp
a mouth poised
to gorge, the eye
pried open, dazed
by the overhead lamp,
its mirror image
a reduced sun
at the pupil's center,
the cornea warped
as beveled glass.
More and more
the world appeared
what Monet painted
in *Les Nymphees*,
all shapes dispersed,
colors' fluid
play disguising
the senses' failure.
Soon doctors
gather as nurses
daub away
emotionless tears,
the laser a light
that tears to heal.

II. *Wisdom Teeth*

Rooted still, half buried
dolmens at the far end
of a henge, these teeth
are in need of excavation,

the ridge a running sore
where some sacrifice
festered below for centuries,
a sickness at the core,

the primitive returned,
those ruminant, wide-eyed
gazers at savannahs
refusing their displacement....

Let them be a keepsake
stored beside a lock of hair,
the opaque gem of your baby incisor
floating on velvet—

these ivory hats with horns.

III. *Splinter*

What hides
under skin
a soul
if it lives
dead thing
in the flesh
a shard
of the cross
black mite
burrowed in
patient wound
till it gnaws
under skin
a thought
bitter shim
of your life
cast away
from the wood
from the *would*
if you lived
differently
dead thing
little pain
not the wound
of the cross
cut it free
from the flesh
see the nail
on the slab—

the moon
of an eye
gone white
gone blind

IV. *Mole*

It appears to appear
from nothing, budding cloud,
slow insurgent, new star;
or has been where it is
from birth, unremarked.

Either way, if it goes
white dwarf, supernova,
it will be what it was—
great serpent, black hole.

Cut it clean, cut it sure,
this brash, incipient,
self-devouring bloom,
toxic blotch, world-swallower,
or nothing at all.

V. *Plantar Wart*

The way weeds spread
through the pliant
garden, sending runners

or tumors splaying
through the body's
wormholes, so these

burls spider across
the sole with each step,
flaring the noxious

sap of their need.
Some say the world
will end in fire, some

in ice—it's ice
then fire: burn
of liquid nitrogen,

acid burn, after which
the wounded foot,
in its instep hush

raw as Philoctetes,
resolved, whispers
Walk on, walk on.

SENIOR CITIZENS' POLKA

That afternoon of my twelfth year
when I wanted to learn guitar
the aged maestro of the neighborhood
—he was ninety if a day
and thin as a Giacometti—

played it, his only published
composition, for me
in the ruined closet of his studio.
I'd rather have riffed
Purple Haze on accordion,

or some other surreal ditty,
jaunty enough to set Beckett
toe-tapping in his Paris
nursing home, *I can't go on,
I'll go on,* the void

scored under every note.
Now I'm fretting over my hairline,
how far my gums will recede.
Eighty years from that summer
I could be a rail myself,

doddering along in a landscape
of trashed alleys and bare trees.
May I kick myself free
of my ashcan, Maestro.
May I also get up and dance.

THE LAY-UP

My father flips a ball
of tissue over the bedrail,
reverse lay-up, deft finger-roll
of wadded spittle swiped
from his chin, from the tube
pumping oxygen where it's taped
into his mouth, another arcing
into his nose where it swills
what appears to be swamp-water
that winds its way through him,
until what passes out again
flows along a catheter
into the glistening sack below.
It's a full court press,
the nagging wires, electrodes
clipped and pasted to his chest,
teams of nurses with their needles—
clot prevention, arterial gas,
bruises tattooing his stomach, arms.
And leaning in where he lifts
his shot: the ventilator,
unshakable defender
hardly breaking a sweat,
pulse an easy rhythmic drum,
his own heart a hummingbird's.
My father's tissue ball swishes
the waste-can's plastic bag.
Two points, I tell him, my fingers
raised in a V. He smiles
through the grimace his breathing tube
has forced his lips into,

its slick curve descending
inside the tunnel of his body,
still, under the soft tarp of sheets.

SAY GRACE

"What's there to eat?"
                    "Hot tongue and cold shoulder,"
a man remarks to his friend
                    as they lower
the shaft of a fencepost into a hole
they've dug in the man's lawn,
                    his friend
belly-laughing while nearby the man's son
watches the work,
                    but doesn't get the joke

until he sees his mother, her face blunt
as the sledge his father wields.

                    It feels
like eons on a family trip, the way
his future reels
                    up to him, parents glum,
an only child staring out the car window

until the boy came to see
                    his life
as curves ahead, sirens gaining, him
speeding to outdistance his pain—

all those years with his fists on the wheel.

So how is it
            now he stands in the glow
of his own kitchen, hooping his arms

around his wife

        where her womb's begun to grow?

"You hungry?" he asks.

          "Let's make dinner."

WEATHER REPORTS

A Red Leaf in Fall

Rivering over the lawn
memos of the earth's hiatus.

A house on a lot on a street—
a woman planting bulbs, her husband

scraping paint from a hull
of weathered clapboards.

And in the chill gust, a boy
with his toy recorder, its

broken note almost buoyant.

After

Now trees are bare
from night's big wind,
leaves chasing leaves,

Dante's lovers
spurred by lust—no,
some cling solely

to the lawn,
shivering hands.
Tomorrow: snow.

GARDEN GLOSSES

I. *Dead Nettle*

And nothing deader in waking spring,
the ground a slab beneath your feet,
these stanched and brittle tubes
like an exposed infrastructure
of pipelines look impossible
to resurrect to former opulence,
the leaves a frosted isinglass,
these white and purple buds,
a pillow-y bed that hurdles the brick
in miraculous slow motion, fond
encroachment on the staid grass
that reclines to suit its charmer.
All summer you'll trim judiciously,
let it be where it wishes to be.

II. *Columbine*

Something of Bosch's fountain
overflowing in Eden,
where the lovers stand unborn

in the glare of the given,
a breath in every blossom,
pink and prelapsarian,

the world-soul, bright and risen
from the source of creation
without a hint of sin—

that carcass rent open
behind it in the background—
nor of anything human.

III. *Delphinium*

Torch, censer, earth's own jewelled staff—
it's as if it pre-existed from time
immemorial in that plastic tray
in *Garden World*, shootlet we nurtured
beside the back fence. We braced
its shaft with splints and rings
until it grew straight, lordly
over columbine and salvia, its blooms
a riotous purple in their own time
uncrowned, shivered loose by wind
the way a child shakes a rattle, petals
nearly weightless when they littered the walk,
no sound, and the bergamot coming on.

IV. *Chives and Thistle*

Starbursts on their edible stalks.
You hardly mind the stray grasses,
those flimsy green flames in the lavender.

Blastocysts teem these other branches,
spiked to pain itself, or pleasure,
truth, beauty, allegorical
and blunt, prickly as Yggdrasil.

V. *Stone Hare*

Ears erect like the one we saw
in Joshua Tree, dead-stopped
on the ridge of a dried out bed
that was sand-trenched and lizard-scurled
beside a crest of brush and yuccas.
How awake he was who startled us.
And so this homage to the real—
its steady, ready stone body,
its soul a poet's or a saint's.

VI. *Forget-Me-Not*

All of you huddled
beside the mossy edge of the stairs
and every sparrow too.

VII. *Fiddlehead Fern*

Pleistocene dreams
beside the backyard hammock
where the patio devolves
    to loam. Weeks ago
their first strivings were corms
        that appeared
    strange eggs below
last fall's rotting draperies—
    those burst seams, those
frail flags faint as whispers,
    while underground more
and still more inroads
    ran along the worm-ways,
    the one life of the many
        medleyed here.
Now this low, verdant umbrage,
    all silk persistence,
shade for the valley lilies
    and their slim perfume.
    Now this green music
        everywhere.

CHIN MUSIC

Whenever I look at this photograph
that hangs beside the bookshelf in my study, I sharpen
my eyes like a batter
who trains on the curveball bending toward the plate,
trying to judge

its spin. And like a curve it seems
to defy physics, how these two once occupied the same
time and space
and still do inside this frame: The Babe as you'd expect
commanding the center,

the rest of the hunting party spreading out
the lesser of the tribe around their chief;
and there, beside him, his hair
slicked back, no longer a wild clownish ring, looking
the young rabbi:

Larry, the lowliest stooge, third fiddle
after Moe and Curly, the straight man whose antic pleas
always seemed more desperate
for having glimpsed the desperate truth. Forget Patroklus;
think instead of Achilles

in love with Caliban, or Gilgamesh
roving out for battle beside Polonius. Think of the Stooges
beside a beefcake Herakles
in a wacky fifties riff on Homeric myth. Or, rather, think
of Everett Brundage

who owned the lodge where this photo
was taken—it had to be sometime in the thirties—
before the Babe's moon-shot drives
arced into legend; before Larry starred with Curly and Moe
in their madcap parody

of Hilter's Germany. I have a tee shirt that reads
"I've seen the future, and it's Fine," where Larry's face
shrieks in neon
as if he'd shaken hands with a thousand volts, his whole head
flashing like an absurd Medusa.

Though when I remember Everett,
I think of a man who for years kept this lodge alive,
a taxidermist's paradise
of deer heads, antlers, bobcats, and one full-size black bear
on the fringe of big resorts.

I remember he had the keenest eyes,
that the whole raucous crowd of locals and exiles
from the city gathered
at his bar, one manifold tribe roaring on into the night.
But I remember, too,

those nights he drank until my father
closed the bar and drove him home; how he lived alone
though he had a wife
who'd left him; how his help—they were friends—stole quietly
from the till,

and he lost the lodge, the one thing he loved.
And whenever I remember how they found him sprawled
dead in the dive
he'd opened on the highway, it makes me think of the phrase
"Chin music,"

meaning a high hard one, a tough pitcher's
brush back of the batter who leans too far over the plate.
"Chin music" was what he said
that afternoon my father drove us down to the lodge
just before it closed.

On TV the pitcher reared into his wind-up,
and swooping down fired a fastball that started letter high,
and rose in a perfect
jet stream directly at the batter's head, driving him to the dirt.
"That's chin music,"

Everett said, leaning his big body
over the bar, his broad nose and wry grin not unlike the Babe's,
"it's how life plays you
before you go down for good." Do I have to say he gave me
the photo for a gift,

that I'm as awestruck now by its sheer
improbability, having watched those stilted newsreels
of the great,
the baffled mania of the stooge who took hammer blows to his head,
who had his eyes

poked out, it seemed, a thousand times?—
the stooges, with their own chin music, that made me think
there was no pain.
In the photograph the turkey splays its feathers before the hunters,
one a hero,

one a thoughtful man who played the fool.
Did Everett take this picture, thrilled to have fame and greatness
come to this unlikely place?
The crowd fans out, mostly smiling, around the kill: Who are
all these nameless men?

UNCHAINED MELODY

One page of the newspaper splays like wings
of a sea gull against the storm-fence raised
around the retreat that was a college
in the last century, before the church
renovated it, and built the old folks home
in the same faux gothic with new cream brick.
I pick up such things, local history,
just by living long enough in one place
and never need to visit the town archives,
or the bookstore on Main, which I do,
to riffle through "the new and gently used"
and banter with the owner when I buy,
or, today, pass through empty-handed
into the street, the names of buildings
still readable on the few preserved facades,
and the memory of the first occupants
more effaced than some peeling billboard
uncovered like one of Pompeii's frescoes
I might read about in a newspaper—
this one, trapped against the chain-link,
a feature in the Metro section beside
Gazebo Nearly Ready For The Fourth;
though it could be headlines, election news,
a house burned in someone else's tragedy,
cars and bikes for sale, furniture and estates,
prom night previews, obits, the sports page
with its important, forgettable scores.
I'd transpose it into a blazing tree,
transfigure it to be a golden bird
or fire-fangled peacock, this urgent scrap,
scavenger flapping madly to ascend

when I happen by, lusty for symbols,
then turn the corner only to hear music
pouring—no lie—from my own house, my wife
singing madrigals—*Adieu, Sweet Amarylis*—
and can almost feel myself beginning
to bleed like so much ink into the earth,
bleed here and now into nothing, and fly.

OF THE HARMONY OF
CELESTIAL REVELATIONS

OF THE HARMONY OF CELESTIAL REVELATIONS

O noblest greenness
who have your roots
in the sun....

—Hildegard Von Bingen

I. *The Reliquary*

Here is the soul, a little golden tent
encased in stone, housing the body's dross
made holy in the foundry of the Word.

Inside its doors, the saint's flesh—tongue
and heart—flames in light beyond all seeing,
guarded by men, their hands frozen in signs,

their eyes erased by the radiance.
There is nothing now for the woman to do
but be the pure flower of her un-being,

while outside vineyards slope to the river
and a wind from the south perfumes the air
and green bells of grapes shake on their stems.

II. *The Cell*

In the beginning is vision—light a fist
to the child's forehead, the sun transplanted
into her soul as into a mirror.

In the beginning is oblation, the child
a tithe her parents offer to the abbess
inside the cathedral's torch-lit ribcage.

In the beginning is the cell—a burial,
the living tomb she vows never to leave,
at seven the child "truly dead to the world."

In the beginning are the Hours, *Opus Dei*,
the works of God sung through days like slates—
At midnight I will rise and give thanks to thee.

III. *The Sickness*

Over again that bright voice, spoken light,
the brain's dazzling scotoma perceived as God—
Ash of ash write what you see and hear,

for forty years her mind a hidden font
of secret mysteries, strange blindnesses
her eyes growing florid in their ecstasy,

the visions indisputably migrainous.
"She experienced a shower of phosphenes
in transit across the visual field."

Then I saw a woman embraced by a tree
wholly dried up, its branches enwound her,
a swarm of clouds where she lay down lamenting.

IV. *The Visions*

In vera luce. First things. The ways of God
scratched into a wax tablet on her knees,
divine gifts poured into the weaker vessel.

Here is the universe, an egg rimmed by fire,
meaning everywhere burns the love of God,
even the outermost haunts of the damned.

God's justice is a grinding stone, his zeal
against the sinner a flying head with wings.
And now appears a Man, his skin sapphire,

jewel-radiant, striding out of the light.
I see these things as in a burning mirror—
the soul and the soul's Life joined at white heat.

V. *The Language*

Blunt code. The tongue's acknowledged ignorance
scrabbled in the spirit's grammatology.
Babel and glossolalia of the soul

the saint mimics from the garbled Word.
And so this *lingua ignota*, language
invented from the speech of the Fallen

pitched to strike the heavenly registers—
Our voice is a coarse burden to the Lord—
while all around significations of leaves,

whole alphabets of stones, assume their forms,
names on a map without territory.
And the river's syntax glistens in the hush.

VI. *The World*

And what of the damned, blighted tenantry
writhing in the steel ardor of the saved?
Here is a lake like a well mouth, its stink

rising, cloud-trains of smoke on the outskirts
of heaven, Truth with its banner stretched out,
emblazoned with the heraldry of the Word.

God's justice is a pike, a burning stone,
the faithless—pigs to be cut in parts.
Above all things God requires our fear.

The saint embraces crusade and pogrom,
I am not worthy to be called a person....
And the chosen soul staggers, calling for blood.

VII. *The Glass*

So let the world be likened unto stained glass,
a rose window born of time and place,
the prism and prison of refracted light

showered from the Unimaginable.
So the light becomes the Word, the Word
the Only-Begotten. So the world becomes

the image we make of it, all we have,
fallen, falsified, saved when we let it go:
the Fall is a fall out of emptiness,

the Word unknowable except by its fall,
Godhead beyond god in the small of the soul,
light within light beyond sight signified.

VIII. *The Healing*

Heat and cold. Earth, fire, water, air.
Causes in the living crux of matter
where the spirit, hidden, alchemies its cures:

For melancholy, compresses of mallow.
For sterility, convolvulus brews.
For desire, ointments of sparrowhawk.

Evil ruts in the demoniac's soul,
a wondrous worm, its sores spawning poison.
But earth is salved by the greenness of earth.

Let the afflicted sup on scraps of her bread.
Let the mad sip from the wine in her cup.
Let newborns pass through girdles of her hair.

IX. *The Greenness*

I am the fire   that keeps the fir
I am the sap   that thrills the womb
I am the murmur   in the blood

I am the ice   that seeds the rose
I am the hawk   beneath the dust
I am the flight   that stills the eye

I am the path   the body hews
I am the tree   that prunes the soul
I am the flood   that flows to God

I am the word   that speaks the flesh
I am the emerald   in the corn
I am the wind   that bears the stone

X. *The Music*

In the beginning all creatures were green,
our voices like Adam's before the Fall,
like these, antiphonal, *Eva* chanted

to *Ave* in dawn light through branching glass.
Notes like perfume, notes like budding gems,
and the world a serpent choking on pearls.

God lives hidden in a woman's body,
a Rose blooming behind the womb's shut door.
Magnificat. The dove's crystal root and salve.

The sky, all sapphire, mirrors the human face,
melisma of time and eternity.
From my wounds I stretch out my Hand to you.

Coda: The Garden

Whitest flower, creation, descendant
from Love's acetylene, and the Word itself
a purple hyacinth—these visions given

to bespeak first things, divine essences,
recede as figures of an unknown tongue
the saint chose to speak as though to angels.

Now, in the garden at day's end, the sun
pours its prodigal light through fluted bells
of columbine, dead nettle, flowering chive,

forget-me-not, a first clematis bloom.
Regard me, I would have it say, *abiding here
among the second things bright and perishing.*

FALL DAY

It is time, Lord. The summer was so immense.
Now on the sundials your shadows stretch their lengths
And across the meadows you release the winds.

Command the last fruits to swell with life,
Grant them still a few days of florid sun,
Press them to completion, and like a hunter
Chase the fleeting sweetness into full-bodied wine.

Whoever has none now will never have a home,
Whoever is alone now will grow lonelier,
Will grow sleepless, reading, scribbling ponderous notes,
And will wander back and forth along the avenues
Restlessly, among the leaves dry and driven.

NOTES

"Fall" is after Rilke's "Herbst" and is dedicated to Linda Dyer, Renata Wood, Marjorie Woodbury, and Michelle Wyrbek.

"The Sea of Time and Space": Some of the details from Blake's life were gleaned from Peter Ackroyd's great biography of the poet.

"Vessels": The Greek word *mythos* means "plot" or "story" and forms the root of the word "myth." The Greek word *pleroma* means "fullness," and refers to a divine cosmic unity embraced by certain Gnostic and Early Christian sects. The Greek word *logos* means "word" and refers to the human's capacity for rational thought. The Greek word *kenosis* means "self-emptying." In Phillipians 2: 5-11, one of the earliest Christian creeds, the word is used to describe the emptying of God's divinity into the humanity of Jesus.

"Marduk": Marduk is the supreme god of the Babylonian pantheon in the *Enuma Elish*.

"Disco Elegy" is for Vinny Savarese, 1958-1976. I am thankful to Barnsley Brown for the idea of a "disco" villanelle.

"In the Bardo of Blue Light": The word "bardo" refers to an intermediate realm between life and death as elaborated in *The Tibetan Book of the Dead*. This poem is for Suzanne Paola, who reminded me that in Tibetan iconography blue light attracts the soul back into the human realm.

"Woman on a Train, Genoa to Paris, 1979": The poem refers to a painting of the Garden of Eden by Lucas Cranach (1472-1553).

"A Cone of the Eucalyptus" is for Mark Solomon.

"Yeats at Balscadden": While in his teens Yeats lived briefly at Balscadden Cottage on Howth, a peninsula jutting into the Irish Sea just north of Dublin. "Paudeen" is Irish slang for "money-grubber."

"Sketching the Galleries": "*Floor Scrapers*" is after Cailbotte; "*A Bather*" is after Degas; "*The Scream*" is after Munch; "*Effigi Tumuli*" is after an earthwork by Michael Heiser; "*Piss Christ*" is after Serrano; "*The Holy Virgin Mary*" is after Ofili; "*Sun in an Empty Room*" is after Hopper.

"Strategies for Turning Away" is dedicated to Stuart Dischell.

"A Fable" is after Aesop's "The Belly and its Members."

"Of the Harmony of Celestial Revelations": Many of the details of the life of St. Hildegard von Bingen (1098-1179) may be found in Sabina Flanagan's *Hildegard of Bingen: A Visionary Life*. Perhaps the greatest of the Rhineland mystics, Hildegard was a visionary, poet, painter, musician, composer, naturalist, healer, and theologian. Oliver Sacks, among others, concluded that Hildegard suffered from migraines, and that her visions have their source in the strange lights that accompanied her attacks. Some of the poem's images derive from Hildegard's work *Scivias (Know the Ways of God)*. *In vera luce*: Latin for "in the light of truth." *Lingua Ignota*: Latin for "unknown language." The phrase refers to a language invented by Hildegard in order to bring human speech closer to the speech of the angels. The title of the poem derives from her symphony for voices of the same title.

"Fall Day" is after Rilke's "Herbsttag."

ACKNOWLDGEMENTS

Grateful acknowledgment is made to the editors of the following publications, where many of these poems first appeared.

The Atlanta Review, The Bellingham Review, Confrontation, Connecticut River Review, Crab Creek, Crania, The Cresset, The Cumberland Review, Georgia Review, Harvard Review, Iron Horse, Jackleg, Mankato Review, The National Forum, The New Renaissance, The Paris Review, Passages North, Ploughshares, Poet Lore, Poetry ("Gilgamesh"), *Poetry East, Prairie Schooner, Prism International, South Dakota Review, The Southern Review, Soundings East, Sou'wester, Yankee, Zone 3.*

"The Sea of Time and Space" and "Vessel: Mythos" were reprinted in *Hammer and Blaze* (University of Georgia Press, 2002); "The Sea of Time and Space" also appears in the online anthology *Enskyment* (www.enskyment.org).

"Floor Scrapers" appears in *The Bread Loaf Anthology of New American Poets* (University Press of New England, 2000).

"The Subway" won second place in the annual Robert Penn Warren Award competition.

"A Bather" won second place in the annual *Yankee Magazine* Poetry competition.

"For Christine at the Frost Farm" appears in *Visiting Frost* (University of Iowa Press, 2005).

"Disco Elegy" appears in *Third Rail: The Poetry of Rock and Roll* (New York: Pocket Books, 2007).

"Wild Stallion, Point Reyes Seashore, 1977" appears in *Cadence of Hooves: A Celebration of Horses* (Yarroway Mountain Press, 2008).

I would also like to thank Sally Ball, Bruce Beasley, Christine Casson, Suzanne Paola, Martha Rhodes, William Thompson, and William Wenthe for their help in revising some of these poems.

This book is dedicated to Tony Behette, Michael Caporlingua, Michael Hardiman, Manny Verdi, and to Christine's garden, for reminding me through the years of the primacy of the second things.